Hats Off to Tea!

Alda Ellis
Artwork by Kathy Hatch

HARVEST HOUSE PUBLISHERS

EUGENE, OREGON

Dedication

To my dear friend Demi, who has traveled the world with me
and always offered her loyal friendship. She is a friend of many talents and has
enlightened me with her expertise in the world of tea.

Alda

HATS OFF TO TEA!
Text Copyright © 2005 by Alda Ellis
Published by Harvest House Publishers
Eugene, Oregon 97402

ISBN-13: 978-0-7369-1490-1
ISBN-10: 0-7369-1490-0

Artwork designs are reproduced under license from © 2005 Kathy Hatch, courtesy of MHS Licensing, and may not be reproduced without permission.

Design and production by Koechel Peterson & Associates, Inc., Minneapolis, Minnesota

Harvest House Publishers has licensed the trade dress rights and the permission to use the words "fun and friendship" from the Red Hat Society for its use on the front cover.

Printed in China

06 07 08 09 10 11 12 13 / LP / 10 9 8 7 6 5 4

To my friend, _____,

May this little book serve as a reminder
that you are special and very important to me.
For you bless so many others
in your warm and caring way.
May the joy you bring to others
return to you today.
God has blessed me with a friend in you.

With love, _____

Contents

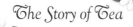

The Story of Tea

Tea has been around for over 5000 years. It is said that water is the world's most popular beverage, but *tea* is second. Tea creates a link between the ancient world and our contemporary traditions. The discovery of tea is credited to Chinese Emperor Shen Nung in 2737 B.C. Even back then, it was common knowledge to boil water to guard against the diseases of the time, and the emperor was certain to do so. The story is told that while making a tour of his provinces, the emperor requested his servants to boil some water for him. A nearby camellia bush provided wood for the fire, and, as a breeze came along, some of the dried leaves from the limbs drifted into the water. Captivated by the aroma wafting from the pot, the emperor drank some of the leaf-flavored water and savored the flavor and the realization that he had stumbled upon a wonderful discovery. Believing that the camellia-leaf water had medicinal qualities, the Chinese began drinking it on a daily basis. Amazingly, we drink virtually the same tea today that Emperor Shen Nung drank the day he discovered it.

Hats Off to Tea
Tea and Friendship—Always in Style

As you don your hat and prepare to attend or host a tea party, I hope this tribute to the ceremony and pleasures of tea serves as inspiration. For all those who share your love of tea, the blending of tea with friendship may be truly found in the cup.

There is hardly the occasion that does not call for tea. A rainy afternoon with a grandchild or two, a neighbor knocking at the back door, a quiet moment of reading curled up with a book, and a celebration of friends and birthdays are all moments just right for a cup of tea. And it seems the fashion of wearing hats has never been more popular than when sipping in the company of friends.

Of course, not everyone has to wear a hat to be proper, but somehow wearing a hat reminds us of another era when it truly was the proper thing to do. Having tea with someone you care about is what's really important. . .for in today's world of telephones, televisions, computers, fax machines, and cellular phones, there is a hunger for a return to graciousness. Hats have the power to open the door of our imagination and transport us to other times and places. Scarlet O'Hara will forever be remembered in her hat with green satin streamers as she teases with Ashley on the sweeping front lawn of Tara. Eliza Dolittle in her straw hat takes us back to Covent Garden, and Katharine Hepburn's sweeping straw hat in *Philadelphia Story* offers a glimpse of pure style.

My little niece Christina has her own box of hats and clothing to dip in to "dress" for her tea parties. She has had tea with her dolls, tea with her mother, tea with friends, and has even hosted a Birthday Tea while they all made grand entrances and exits in their hats. But we don't have to be little to appreciate dressing up for teatime.

The Story of Tea

The very first teapots were fashioned after the Chinese little pot that was actually mundanely used for water. It took several centuries for the teapot to evolve as we know it today. The Chinese discovered that if they covered the tea when they steeped it, it produced a richer flavor and a lid was created to keep the heat in. It was even discovered that the

Hats offer a glimpse into another side of our personality. Just as an actor dresses in his costume and begins to step into his character, we can place a hat upon our head and step into a moment of make-believe. Perhaps hats have made us feel a bit queenly and show a more elegant side to our personality. When we think of the real Queen of England, we immediately picture her donning hat and gloves rather than her jewel encrusted crown. The "Queen of Camelot" in America, Jacqueline Kennedy, will forever be romantically remembered in her perfectly tailored pillbox hat.

While coffee may have many devotees in the contemporary workday world, a cup of tea raised to lips shaded beneath the brim of a classic hat is a tribute to the elegance of the past. With such action we evoke a gentler time and place; we recall a childhood escape, the starlets of Hollywood, and the heroines of classic literary tales. A beautiful, inspiring hat and a cup of tea with friends can transform the everyday into a richer, most memorable occasion.

In my daily life, taking tea is a way to revisit traditions and memories of my youth. Like so many, I grew up drinking iced tea (that my mother made in a glass gallon jug) and drank hot tea on cold mornings or at special parties. My mother prepared tea every day while I was growing up. With the sweltering Southern summers, our family could go

type of clay that the teapot was made from made a difference in developing the flavor of the tea. So as the tea made its way from the Far East to the European West on the grand trading clipper ships of the day, the teapots and teawares became part of the Oriental treasures for the upper class and nobility.

through a gallon a day! Mother always made it in the evening so it could be refrigerated overnight and ready for the next day. I still have the green enamel pan that she used to brew her tea.

My cousin Beth says her tea drinking has evolved over her lifetime. "As all Southern girls, I grew up drinking tea. 'Ice tea'... not 'iced tea,' which may be the proper way to say it. More specifically, Lipton ice tea, which was often called Lipton Tea ... as in 'would you like a glass of Lipton tea?' The ice tea in my home was made by the gallons. Around noon, mama or the housekeeper, Lisa, would boil a large cast aluminum pot of water that they would pour over several large tea bags in

Teapot or Teakettle?

The difference between a tea-kettle and a teapot is that a *kettle* is used to boil water in and is usually made of metal. The *teapot* is used for serving on the tea table and is made of silver, porcelain, china, or pottery. Silver and stainless steel are the only metals that will not distort the tea's flavor.

a gallon glass jar. I assume we owned a pitcher that we used when we had company, but I only remember the large gallon jar. The tea would often be hot when it was poured into the tall glasses of ice and often it wasn't until your third helping of ice before it was really ice tea.

"Sugar and quartered lemons were always on the table for all that wanted sugar or lemon . . . and everyone always did. And as far as I knew, restaurants only served sweetened tea and no one was ever offered an option."

Well, today there are options, all sorts of options. Herbal teas (which are not real teas at all) to designer teas, traditional black **teas, green** teas, white tea, artistic teas that bloom, chai teas, and the hip Taiwan**ese bubbl**e tea (that has pearls of tapioca added and is served with a fat straw) are **all wonder**ful choices.

And after all these years of taking tea at the Ritz Carlton in **Atlanta, T**he Drake in Chicago, the boutique hotels of London, The Peninsula in **Hong Kong,** or the Taj Mahal hotel in New Delhi, I still find that my favorite tea is the **orange** pekoe that my sweet mother brewed in that old green battered enamel pan.

*The tea equipage is usually placed upon a silver-salver
or china kettle on a stand and the cups are small.
Thin bread and butter, cake, petit-fours and sometimes
fresh fruit are all the eatables given. These are
daintily arranged on plates, spread with lace doilies
and placed in a cake stand or on a convenient table.*

MRS. BEETON
The Book of Household Management

Home Is a Friend and a Cup of Tea

Tea has long been the perfect accompaniment to the special moments of
our lives, and even though I have been drinking tea all of my life, I recently
discovered the *world* of tea. While traveling on a business trip to India with
my good friend Demi, we took pause of our day to sample all sorts of different
teas... and I think I found the secret to its 5000-year-old success. The ceremony
of tea illuminates a memorable moment shared between friends.

Hats Off to a Perfect Pot of Tea

 Start by filling the teakettle with fresh cold water.

 Bring the kettle to a quick boil, and warm the teapot by swishing a bit of hot water inside and pouring it out.

 If using teabags, place your teabags in the pot and pour the almost boiling water over them.

 If using loose tea, still add the tea first and pour the water over the tea (one scoop of loose tea for every person plus one for the pot).

 Steep by letting it sit for three to five minutes. Brew by the time and not the color (for certain, no more than five minutes). Remove the tea leaves or bags or the tea will be bitter.

 If adding lemon, place the slice of lemon in the bottom of the cup and pour the tea over it.

 If taking milk, add it to the cup first and then add the tea. (Never add milk to green or oolong teas.)

 Add sugar or honey if desired.

 Serve white granulated sugar or sugar cubes in a sugar bowl. Tongs are used with cubes and a sugar spoon with granulated sugar. Brown sugar is reserved for coffee.

Demi and I found ourselves in the midst of a country that has been known for generations of its tea industry and is recognized as the world's largest exporter of tea. We were weary travelers pausing a moment to take off our hats that protected us from the sun. Steep mountainsides of lush greenery revealed the actual tea bushes and offered up the country's richest treasure. The tea grown high in the clouds at the foothills of the Himalayan Mountains was prepared for us as we chose different blends to widen our horizons.

Cupping our hands, we drank from the smooth porcelain, yet somehow it was the warmth of the company that made it so memorable. We were thousands of miles from home, and tea became the poignant ceremony that reminded us of family and everything that we held dear...including each other. I hope that **you too** will become even more immersed in the world's most **popular beverage** and all it offers... and together we can say, **"Hats off to** tea!"

Candy Oranges

 1 can Eagle Brand sweetened condensed milk
2 tablespoons homogenized milk
1 cup powdered sugar
2 packages (3 ounces each) orange flavored gelatin

 1 pound flaked coconut, finely ground
1 cup almonds, finely ground
orange food coloring
green decorator prepared icing with leaf tip
slivered almonds

Combine sweetened condensed milk, homogenized milk, powdered sugar, 1 package of orange flavored gelatin, ground coconut, and ground almonds. Mix well. Add a few drops of orange food coloring. Refrigerate until firm enough to shape.

Form mixture into small, walnut-sized balls. Roll each one in reserved orange flavored gelatin. Add stems made from almond slivers. With green icing, pipe a single leaf at the base of each almond sliver. Store in covered containers at room temperature.

These may be made ahead of time and frozen for up to a month. Makes about 25 to 30 oranges. Serve on a silver tray lined with real shiny washed dark green leaves.

Girls in Their Pearls
A Classic Tradition

The chef at the Ritz Carlton once told me, "We eat with our eyes." So whether tea is served for two or for twenty, the presentation is an important part of the experience. At the turn of the eighteenth century, the status symbol of England was an elegant silver tea service with all of the accessories, and now they are used on mostly special occasions. Part of the enjoyment of tea is in the pleasure of the ritual that is still enhanced by beautiful presentation.

Today it seems there has been a revival of tea parties and the rules have certainly changed. Women in hats—especially those girls in red hats—have been making a showing all over. When I was growing up, my mother taught me that the only thing really important for us girls to wear whether we were six or sixty was our pearls. Almost any outfit could be tea-party worthy if we wore our pearls. Gloves and hats are still

proper no matter what age, but certainly not required. We have all grown to realize that the most important thing we wear to a tea party is simply a warm heart and a friendly smile.

In preparing for a tea party, I am always reminded of the story of Martha in the Bible. She was the sister of Mary and Lazarus. Jesus was coming as their guest, and Martha fussed over the preparation details. And, it turned out, she was so busy fussing in her kitchen during His visit that she almost missed out on the opportunity to enjoy His company. Meanwhile, her sister, Mary, was spending important time talking with Jesus and savoring the time in His presence. With that story in mind, I keep my guests as my focus. I shouldn't fret about whether I have the perfect kitchen, brand-new decorations, or a complete matching set of my favorite china. When we feel we must have everything in order or everything coordinated "just so," it takes away from our ability to share

Scones and Devonshire Cream

Scones are essentially a light biscuit, only sweet. There are so many recipes and variations on a traditional recipe, but I will share my secret. I use a ready-made mix that all I add is water for the dough. This is quick and easy, especially after working all day.

Gourmet food stores and some grocery stores offer very nice commercial mixes which are found next to the biscuit mix. Toss in a handful of chopped pecans or white chocolate morsels, cranberries, raisins, or orange zest, and you have "homemade" scones . . . just don't

our hearts and prevents us from sharing those mismatched, delightful pieces we have acquired . . . the ones that actually make a tea gathering a true classic.

My mismatched teacups are treasured because each one holds a story of a special friend or place, and they hold a message of comfort and welcome. Dressing the tea table is especially fun for me. I simply adore all the accessories of tea and find them irresistible. Sugar tongs, tea knives, and butter butlers link us to the past yet connect us to the ceremony of tea with grace and charm. Sitting down and taking tea with the accoutrements is all part of the ceremony and pleasure. Some of my treasures have been passed down through my family, but most have been purchased during side trips when I travel for business. As a collector, I get such a thrill when discovering a wonderful

tea strainer, sugar spoon, or lemon fork that has been used to serve and connect people over the years. These individual keepsakes make elegant table favors when tied with a sheer French ribbon. Tuck in a place card for a seated tea.

Cups used by nobility could not be valued any more than my varied collection. You don't have to have a complete silver tea service to prepare for a charming tea. There are great finds to be had at flea markets, tag sales, and antique stores. My mother-in-law was going to toss out a lusterware cream and sugar bowl. I exclaimed, "I would love to have that!" Another favorite find of mine is a yard sale creamer in the shape of a little white cow that when you hold his tail and tilt him, the cream is dispensed through his mouth. They used to be in everyone's cupboard,

tell everything you know. Serve scones warm, right out of the oven, so the butter will melt with strawberry jam and Devonshire cream.

Each little bowl of jam, clotted cream, or Devonshire cream should have its own little spoon in it.

Southern Devonshire Cream

- 1 6-ounce carton sour cream
- 1 8-ounce block of cream cheese
- 1 cup powdered sugar

Cream ingredients together and beat with an electric mixer until light and fluffy. Serve in a beautiful crystal bowl. Garnish with a strawberry and snippet of mint.

but a plain white one is hard to find. I am sure thrift stores are also full of treasures waiting to be found.

The settings of our table link us with the past tradition of taking tea. Varied patterns among dessert plates make for interesting conversation for the guests who are just getting acquainted. Most of us don't have the time or the skill to create the delicate embroidery and crochet patterns like our mothers and grandmothers knew by heart, so antique linens are a wonderful collection to begin or grow. But the most important thing to remember when gathering your own tea accessories is to gather items that have meaning. Don't choose one that is worth a lot . . . choose the piece you simply fall in love with.

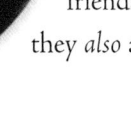

I have even been known to ask friends to bring their own teacups, but they *also* are supposed to bring a story

There is a great deal of poetry
and fine sentiment in a chest of tea.

RALPH WALDO EMERSON

with the cup to share with the rest of us. This is especially enjoyable when some of the guests might not know each other.

Whether we dress up or not is not what matters, the priority is getting together with friends. Remember, too, that a tea party at a hotel or a charming little tearoom is a great way to catch up with friends because then each lady can be a "Mary" instead of a "Martha."

Sour Cream Sugared Almonds

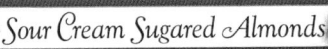

 ½ cup sour cream

1½ cups sugar

 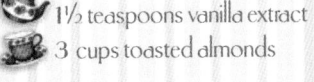 1½ teaspoons vanilla extract

3 cups toasted almonds

Mix cream and sugar together. With a candy thermometer heat mixture to 223°, stirring constantly. Add vanilla and nuts. With a wooden spoon, stir rapidly until the mixture has coated all the nuts. Spread on a waxed-paper-lined cookie sheet and separate the nuts. Cool thoroughly and store in an airtight container until ready to enjoy. These may be made up to two months ahead of time and stored in the refrigerator.

Travels with Tea

While in London . . .

Late in the seventeenth century, over 500 coffeehouses existed in London. Women were traditionally not allowed in coffeehouses, and it was not until 1717 that Thomas Twining opened the first English tearoom strictly for women. On a trip to London, I visited the original Twining's teashop as it is still operating today at 216 Strand Street. If you are ever traveling nearby, I encourage you to make a stop and take a sip on behalf of women everywhere.

Most delightful!

Special Delivery

When you are preparing for a special party, arrange a pretty plate of goodies and cover it with plastic wrap. After your party is over, take the treats to a shut-in and share with her (or him) the spirit of your party. Add a couple of teabags and make the tea for her while you are there. Making someone feel special makes the lonely feel loved. My good friend Mr. Dan once told me that you could forget what someone once said, but you could never forget the way they made you feel. Make someone feel special. Little things are long remembered.

The Story of Tea

One of the reasons that tea became more affordable in continental Europe is that it became more available. In the early 1800s, the East India Trading Company discovered that tea actually grew wild in Assam, which is the northern part of India. With faster ships and the establishment of new tea plantations, tea became affordable to the masses. Some of those tea plantations that were formed are still in operation today.

Brimming Over with Joy
The Gift of Hospitality

Little acts of kindness offering compassion, companionship, and courtesy let someone know they are special. The most cherished part of a tea for me is opening my heart and serving the gift of friendship. A thoughtful way to welcome someone new, make someone feel special, show someone they will be missed, or let a lonely heart know they are not alone is to offer a simple cup of tea.

Through the years my collection of teapots and china has grown, but each piece is a reminder of someone dear or someplace special. Some of the plates I use primarily for decoration. Such was the case with one very special dessert plate adorned with roses. The china pattern was one I had never seen before. When I stumbled across it during a trip, its dainty design captured my heart. I gave it a temporary home on my wall display, hoping that eventually it could join the rest of a set. "Bavaria" was encircled on the back, so I knew it must be quite old. Apparently it was not only old but hard to find. My search over two years resulted in nothing.

One night after a summer's evening party, my friend from church stayed late to help me do the dishes. When she looked at the display on my wall, she nearly dropped the goblet in her hands. "That was my grandmother's china pattern. I haven't seen it since I was a little girl," she exclaimed.

Instinctively I reached up and pulled the plate from the wall. I just knew that this moment was the reason I had found the plate. It was going home.

On a business trip to Hong Kong, a friend and I were enjoying breakfast at The Peninsula, one of the most luxurious hotels in the world. With our newly purchased postcards, we sat down in a little café overlooking the lobby. As we sat and penned a few greetings, we took time to admire the peaceful surrounding fountains and architecture. The crisply dressed waiter came and jotted down our order. My friend and I looked up to take in a huge, sculptured marble balcony overhead. It held a dozen or so members of a symphony orchestra that, much to our delight, were preparing to play.

27

Creating an Ice Ring

A beautiful ice ring filled with flowers in the center of the punchbowl is that extra little detail to make a tea most memorable. To make an ice ring, use boiled water, so there will not be any air bubbles in the ring and it will be crystal clear. Fill a bundt cake pan one third full of water and place assorted fresh flowers. Freeze.

Fill a second time and freeze again.

To release the ring when ready to serve, simply run under warm water for a few seconds.

The waiter brought our croissants and tea on an elegant silver tray. I recall that this was the first time I had been offered a simple syrup mixture rather than granulated or cubed sugar. This sweet treat was served in an exquisite silver pot. We savored each bit of this foreign hospitality as the musicians above began to play. After just a couple of notes, I understood that music truly is the universal language; here we sat thousands of miles from home at that Sunday breakfast tea, and the musicians began to play a tune my spirit knew by heart: "Amazing Grace." Oh, how sweet the sound.

Serving from the Heart

When I was growing up, my mother used to have tea parties for her friends. She would set up the card table in our living room and drape it with a freshly starched white linen cloth. The dessert plates, teacups, and our Sunday dishes were brought out of the china closet and made ready for tea. Fresh roses were picked from the bush that covered our fence to create a perfect centerpiece, and Mother's beautifully laundered, hand-embroidered napkins were folded neatly and placed on the table. I was too young to be in school, so Mother invited me as a guest.

One of Mother's tea parties made such an impression on me. Her fragrant, old-fashioned pink roses were picked and placed at each of three place settings. . . one for me, one for Mother, and one for our guest.

The Story of Tea

The word *caddy* was from the Chinese word *catty*, for one pound weight. Though its usage has been transformed to mean a container today, even now a tea caddy should hold about one pound of tea.

The care spent on the details was just as she had always done. The humble, little card table was transformed into a beautiful setting for tea and a special guest. The doorbell rang, and Mother's friend arrived needing a little help to the table. Her son had brought her to the party and he quickly ran back to his running car. I remember sitting at the table rather quiet that day, listening to the ladies visit back and forth and holding Mother's smooth china teacup in my hand. I just kept thinking about all the trouble my mother went to in making such a beautiful table for tea . . . not one detail overlooked. You see, our guest of honor that day had placed under the card table her thin white cane.

That tea party taught me that with all the things seen and unseen, friendship is felt with the heart. Sometimes we are saddened when a friend that we have grown to love has to move far away. A neighborhood tea is a thoughtful way to let several of the neighbors or co-workers offer a last good-bye. It is said, "Tea tames tears and thirst."

My favorite cousin's family was in the military and moved a lot. We were the same age, and we kept in touch through letters no matter where she was. Her tea set traveled the world, and home became wherever she and her mother unpacked the cups, saucers, and teapot. She told me how much her mother loved tea parties because other military wives could understand the heartaches that went with the job. Even though the military base would host warm and welcoming parties with gleaming silver urns and elegant fare, it was the smaller, more personal teas that filled and welcomed, consoled and warmed her heart.

Through her letters, my cousin taught me the pain of moving and leaving behind friendships just beginning. There were long, dangerous tours of duty and heart-wrenching good-byes. This deeper understanding of the sorrow such a move creates helps me be more sensitive to those old and new friends who are torn from their loved ones.

There are a host of reasons to, well…host a tea. You might welcome a new family to your neighborhood or say good-bye to an old friend; share the joy of a new life or the pain of a recent loss; celebrate a wedding or honor an anniversary. These special occasions can be made more meaningful and memorable with a thoughtful gesture of hosting a tea and treating each guest to a parting gift. "A gift to remember me by"—what thoughtful words. A gift of a teacup and saucer to be remembered by is always thoughtful, but sometimes there are even more personal gestures.

As a parting gift for a gardening friend, I once gathered acorns from my oak tree and placed them in a small paper bag filled with a nest of sphagnum moss. I included a note encouraging them to plant the acorns and they will soon root to have a fledgling oak tree to remind them of what they left behind. Meaningful gifts that speak to another's heart and soul will forever be remembered.

Little things do make a difference.
Will you be the rock that redirects the stream?
ALDA ELLIS

Travels with Tea

Memories of India . . .

Recently I visited a wonderful little tea shop in New Delhi, India. The shop owner, Mr. Mittal, shared with me the fact that his region of the country is the world's largest tea-producing province in the world and the tea grown there has an ideal combination of taste and aroma, making it a tea more prized than Darjeeling in some countries. Mr. Mittal said that where, when, and how tea was grown affected the flavor.

Yet, how the leaves are harvested has an even greater impact on the end product. When the leaves are dried and processed, they become what is known as black tea. Just like in the world of wine, the different teas are named for a region of the country. Thus, Assam tea comes from Assam province of India and Darjeeling tea comes from Darjeeling. Now I love to sip my tea and imagine or recall memories of the place where my savory cup first developed its flavor and aroma.

Sweet Memories Tea

Pecan Tea Cookies

Apricot Balls

Cucumber Sandwiches

Herbed Cheese and Smoked Salmon Sandwiches

Chess Cake

Southern Tea Punch

Apricot Balls

🎩 1 can Eagle Brand milk
(sweetened condensed milk)

🎩 16 ounces ground apricots

🎩 3 cups coconut

🎩 powdered sugar

In a large mixing bowl, combine milk, apricots, and coconut. Mix well and roll into one-inch balls. Roll in powdered sugar. Let air dry completely before storing in an airtight container. Serve in a pedestal bowl lined with a doily.

Pecan Tea Cookies

These cookies have a melt-in-your-mouth buttery flavor. They are nice to place in a gift box lined with waxed paper and tied with a beautiful satin ribbon. What a treat to eat in the car or on the plane, and the recipient knows they are loved!

🎩 1 cup (2 sticks) butter

🎩 ½ cup sugar

🎩 1 teaspoon vanilla extract

🎩 2 cups all-purpose flour, sifted before measuring

🎩 ½ teaspoon salt

🎩 2 cups finely chopped pecans

🎩 powdered sugar

Preheat oven to 300°.

Cream butter, sugar, and vanilla together until fluffy. Sift flour with salt and add to cream mixture, blending thoroughly. Add pecans and mix well. Shape into small rolls 1½ inches long and place on non-stick cookie sheet.

Bake for 20 minutes.

Do not brown. Cool, and then roll in powdered sugar. Store in loosely covered container to assure that the cookies retain their crispness. This recipe makes about 60 cookies and may be made ahead of time and frozen.

Herbed Cheese and Smoked Salmon Sandwiches

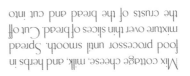

- 1 cup small curd cottage cheese
- 2 teaspoons milk
- 1 tablespoon chopped parsley
- 1/2 teaspoon ground pepper
- 1/4 teaspoon thyme
- 1/2 clove garlic, peeled
- tea sandwich bread
- smoked salmon, thinly sliced

Mix cottage cheese, milk, and herbs in food processor until smooth. Spread mixture over thin slices of bread. Cut off the crusts of the bread and cut into triangle fourths by cutting an "x" into the bread. Top each sandwich with a slice of smoked salmon and a garnish such as a snip of parsley, dill, or other fresh herb.

Traditional Cucumber Sandwiches

- 1 loaf thinly sliced white bread
- 8 ounces cream cheese
- 1 large cucumber, seeded and grated
- 1 small onion, grated
- 1 cup mayonnaise
- a dash of lemon pepper

Remove crusts from bread. Mix cream cheese, cucumber, onion, and mayonnaise. Spread onto bread to make sandwiches and add a dash of lemon pepper. Quarter sandwiches into small triangles and, before serving, top each piece with a tiny sprig of rosemary...for remembrance.

Chess Cake

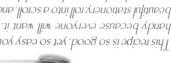

This recipe is so good, yet so easy you will make it often. Be sure to have the recipe handy because everyone will want it. You might even want to photocopy it onto beautiful stationery, roll into a scroll, and tie with a satin ribbon as a way for the guests to remember the special tea and the guest of honor.

- 1 box lemon cake mix
- 3 eggs
- ⅓ cup butter, melted
- 8 ounces cream cheese
- 1 box powdered sugar
- 1 teaspoon vanilla extract

Preheat oven to 350°. Mix lemon cake mix, 1 egg, and butter. Press in the bottom of a 9" x 12" pan. Mix cream cheese, 2 eggs, powdered sugar, and vanilla, spread over bottom layer. Bake for 45 to 50 minutes.

Optional: Decorate each piece with a sugared pansy. To make these, simply coat a fresh washed pansy with egg white and sprinkle with sugar. Let dry on wax paper.

Tea Roses

In Europe, around the mid-1800s, a particular group of roses was given the name *Tea Roses*. It is thought they were given the name because they smelled like a newly opened tin of tea, for most of the tea imported to England in those days was perfumed with flowers.

Southern Tea Punch

Depending on how many guests are expected at your tea, you might want to think about serving a tea punch for convenience sake. If it is just a few neighbors dropping by, you might go ahead and ready the teapots, but if it is a group of ten or more, a tea punch is quite appropriate. My mother made a tea punch that was so delicious everyone wanted her recipe. I am happy to share it with you.

🫖 2-quarts brewed tea (orange pekoe)

🫖 1½ cups sugar

🫖 12 oz. can frozen grape juice

🫖 12 oz. can frozen pineapple juice

Stir together tea, sugar, grape juice, and pineapple juice. Pour into gallon-size container and add enough water to make one gallon. Refrigerate and serve cold over ice. Garnish glasses with a sprig of mint.

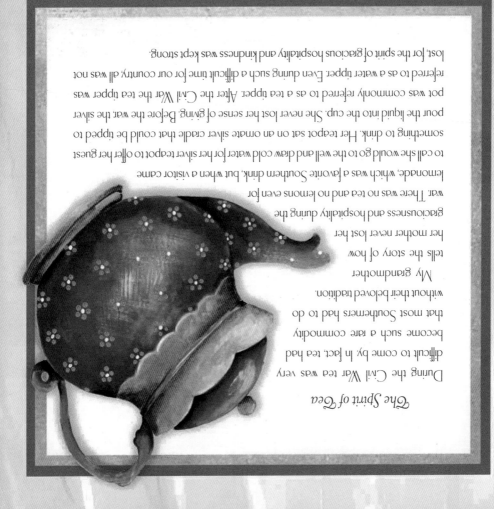

The Spirit of Tea

During the Civil War tea was very difficult to come by. In fact, tea had become such a rare commodity that most Southerners had to do without their beloved tradition.

My grandmother tells the story of how her mother never lost her graciousness and hospitality during the war. There was no tea and no lemons even for lemonade, which was a favorite Southern drink, but when a visitor came to call she would go to the well and draw cold water for her silver teapot to offer her guest something to drink. Her teapot sat on an ornate silver cradle that could be tipped to pour the liquid into the cup. She never lost her sense of giving. Before the war, the silver pot was commonly referred to as a tea tipper. After the Civil War the tea tipper was referred to as a water tipper. Even during such a difficult time for our country, all was not lost, for the spirit of gracious hospitality and kindness was kept strong.

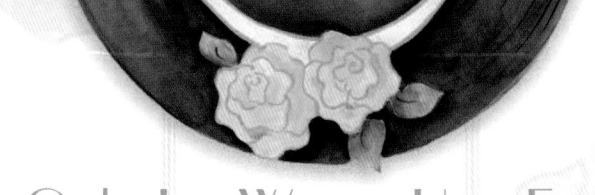

Girls Just Want to Have Fun
Celebrations Among Friends

*T*ea societies have been around since the eighteenth century, and today there seems to have been a return to the popularity of such organizations and others. The attraction is simple…women enjoy the company of other women. We understand each other. We find it perfectly normal for one woman to own six pairs of black shoes. We can distinguish the subtle differences between cream, white, and ivory. And we completely understand that it is okay to cry because we are so *happy*.

A just-for-fun tea party allows us to connect with one another. Around a relaxing, inviting table we can laugh at ourselves, cry with each other, vent our frustrations, and share our defeats and successes. The most thoughtful thing you can do for your guests is let them know how happy you are to be with them.

Katharine Hepburn has been quoted as saying, "If you obey all the rules, you will miss all the fun." Don't be concerned with too many details or if you are doing everything just perfect. Leave that to the Victorians—they were concerned with all the proper dress and proper utensils. It is reported that at one time some silverware sets included over two hundred pieces for each intricate detail such as berry spoons, asparagus tongs, and pickle forks. Today what is proper and best is to put the emphasis on your guests, and everything else will fall into place.

When entertaining the idea of honoring a friend's birthday, homecoming, or special accomplishment, don't let hosting a tradi-tional tea become overwhelming. A simple

The Story of Tea

In its early days tea was such an expensive luxury that it was guarded quite carefully. It was kept in delicate intricate little jars and stored under lock and key. Even though the servants would ready the tea table for tea, the actual tea itself was stored in the parlor or the room that it was to be served in, and always under the watchful eye of the lady of the house.

Bring out your mother's or grandmother's tea cart. A tea cart is most helpful and can be rolled into the room where you are serving. If you don't have one, look for a vintage one, for they make a tea party more festive when decorated with ivy and ribbons. More than anything, they give you more space where it is needed to actually serve the tea.

When hosting a tea party in your home, remember that some guests will use your bathroom before they leave for home. Fill the bathtub with water and sprinkle pink rose petals in the water. Add two or three floating candles.

way to remember it is classically with a three-course meal: sandwiches, scones, and desserts, and all served with little extras such as jams, clotted cream, and honey. Within this simple menu a tea can be presented in your own creative way.

On a Friday night, think about hosting a pajama party. The rewards are double for this kind of party, for you get the pleasure in planning it and the pleasure when you actually have it. Ask everyone to wear their wildest pajamas. Find an old record player and ask everyone to bring those albums that they haven't listened to in years. Perhaps hire a manicurist to give everyone the luxury of getting their nails done, or provide a basket of foot

creams and lotions with white fluffy towels tied up with French ribbons. These little luxuries provide wonderful ice breakers to get to know each other for the first time or once again. Pass around a card for everyone to sign for the one special friend who was not able to attend and let her know she was missed. Award a prize for the wildest house slippers.

When hosting a casual tea, it is helpful to select foods that are easy to serve. Avoid messy foods that require too much silverware. Food that can be picked up and eaten with the fingers is most appropriate and convenient at this kind of gathering. Use plates that are large enough to keep food from spilling on the floor, and designate a location where plates and teacups can be placed when they are finished. Several large trays are especially nice for this duty.

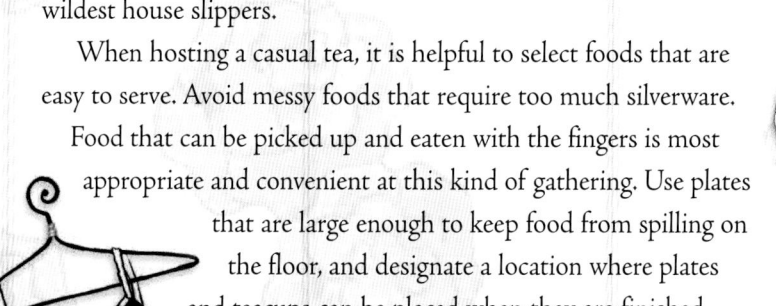

In addition to a Pajama Party tea, other great Girls' Night In themes are Darlin' Divas or a Spa tea. No matter which theme you choose or invent, have several disposable cameras around for guests to take candid shots that can be laughed at now and again. You will probably think of

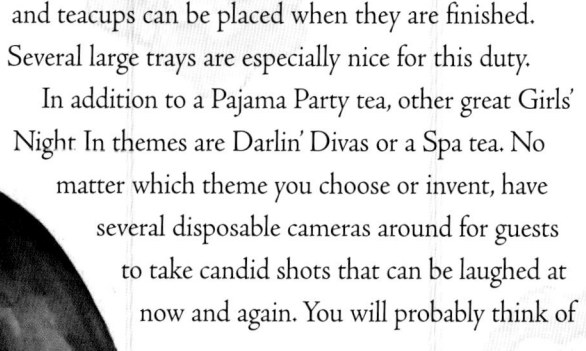

other ideas to liven up such a party. The atmosphere at this kind of gathering releases the tension of the work week. The warmth of tea and friendship is a wonderful way to entertain and is especially welcoming in an increasingly frenzied world. As time goes by, tuck in the picture of your guest with a handwritten note letting her know how much you appreciate her coming. It is the thoughtful little things that truly warm the heart.

Rose Petal Sugar

For an afternoon tea, Rose Petal Sugar is pretty to look at and makes the sugar even sweeter with its delicate fragrance. Layer individual petals from unsprayed roses and alternate with granulated sugar. Close the lid tightly on the jar and let it rest in the cupboard for a few weeks. When ready to use, sift out the rose petals and serve the sugar in a crystal pedestal sugar bowl. Add one or two fresh petals as garnish for the sugar. Store unused sugar in an airtight container.

A pyramid of assorted cakes
will be more immediately attractive
and give more satisfaction
than an elaborately ornamented cake on which
two to three days' work has been put.

JESSUP WHITEHEAD
The Steward's Handbook, 1893

A Girls' Night In Tea

Petite Chocolate Chip Cheesecakes

Lemon Curd Squares

Rosemary Chicken Salad

Cheesy Pecan Toast Triangles

Olive-Filled Cheese Balls

Fresh Apple Cake

For hot tea. Gather a selection of specialty teas, so each guest can try something that maybe they have not tried before.

For iced tea. Brew a favorite iced tea blend and offer lots of lemon wedges.

(Remember, for hot tea, lemon is sliced in rounds. For iced tea, lemon is always served as wedges.)

Petite Chocolate Chip Cheesecakes

- 1 8-ounce block of cream cheese, softened
- 3/4 cup sugar
- 2 eggs
- 1 tablespoon lemon juice
- 1 teaspoon vanilla
- 1 cup mini semi-sweet chocolate chips
- 24 vanilla wafers

Beat cream cheese, sugar, eggs, lemon juice, and vanilla until light and fluffy. Add the mini chocolate chips and mix well. Line muffin pans with paper liners. Put one vanilla wafer in each. Fill each cup about two-thirds full. Bake at 375° for 15 minutes or until ever-so-lightly browned around the edges. Let the cheesecakes cool and then drizzle with chocolate (see below).

Makes 24 petite cheesecakes.

Chocolate Drizzle. In a heavyweight Ziplock bag, melt 1 cup of regular semi-sweet chocolate chips. Once the chips have melted, cut a tiny hole in one corner of the bag. Drizzle melted chocolate over tiny cheesecakes. Garnish with a fresh raspberry on top of each one.

Lemon Curd Squares

2 sticks butter, softened
2 cups all-purpose flour
3/4 cup powdered sugar
4 eggs

2 cups granulated sugar
6 tablespoons lemon juice
1 tablespoon flour
1/2 teaspoon baking powder

Preheat oven to 325°.

Mix butter, flour, and powdered sugar and press into 10" x 14" pan. Bake for 15 minutes.

Beat eggs slightly, then add sugar, lemon juice, 2 tablespoons flour, and baking powder. Mix and pour on top of pastry. Bake at 325° for 40 to 50 minutes.

Upon removing from the oven, sprinkle with additional powdered sugar. Cool and cut into squares. Serve each lemon square with a fresh strawberry fanned on top for garnish.

Earl Grey Tea

The favored Earl Grey tea is named after a nineteenth-century British diplomat to China, where he learned to enjoy the orange-scented tea blend that still bears his name. Earl Grey tea is scented with the oil of bergamot fruit, which resembles a Mediterranean orange.

Rosemary Chicken Salad Croissants

 3 cups cooked chicken breast, cubed

 3 cups celery, thinly sliced

⅓ cup mayonnaise

⅓ cup sour cream

1 tablespoon fresh rosemary, finely chopped

Combine chicken and celery. In a separate bowl, blend mayonnaise, sour cream, and rosemary. Fold in chicken with dressing and mix until coated.

Place a heaping tablespoon of chicken salad onto the bottom half of ready-baked miniature croissants. Place the top on, and decorate the serving tray with sprigs of fresh rosemary, red grapes, and pink roses.

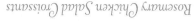

Cheesy Pecan Toast Triangles

-  2 pounds sharp cheddar cheese, shredded
- ½ stick butter, softened
- ¼ cup mayonnaise
- 1 tablespoon fresh lemon juice
- 2 cups lightly toasted pecans, finely chopped
- salt
- Tabasco, to taste
- 8 pieces toasted white bread, crusts trimmed
- finely chopped green onions
- pimento stuffed olives

Toast pecans ever so lightly by placing them on a cookie sheet for 5 to 7 minutes at 350°. Stir often.

Remove the pecans from the oven, and preheat the broiler.

In a small bowl, mix together the cheese, butter, mayonnaise, lemon juice, pecans, salt, and dash of Tabasco to taste. Spread the mixture on the toast and broil until it is bubbly and pulled . . . only 1 or 2 minutes. Sprinkle green onions on top of each one. Cut into triangles and garnish with a pimento stuffed olive on each one and serve.

Fresh Apple Cake

- 2 eggs
- 1 cup oil
- 2 cups sugar
- 3 cups flour
- 2 teaspoons cinnamon
- 2 teaspoons soda
- 2 teaspoons salt
- 3 cups diced apples
- 1/2 cup nuts

Preheat oven to 350°. In large mixing bowl, beat eggs, stir in oil. In a second bowl, sift the flour, cinnamon, soda, and salt all together and slowly add to egg mixture. Stir in the apples and nuts. Bake for about 40 minutes or until a knife comes out clean.

Serve on pedestal cake stand, and garnish with fresh flowers.

Olive Filled Cheese Balls

- 1 cup sharp cheddar cheese, shredded
- 2 tablespoons butter
- 1/2 cup all-purpose flour
- dash cayenne pepper
- 20 medium garlic stuffed olives

Cream together cheese and butter. Blend in the flour and cayenne. Wrap a teaspoonful of dough around each olive; squeeze them in the palm of your hand. Cover the olive completely. Place on non-stick cookie sheet and bake at 400° for 12 to 15 minutes. This recipe yields about 20 balls.

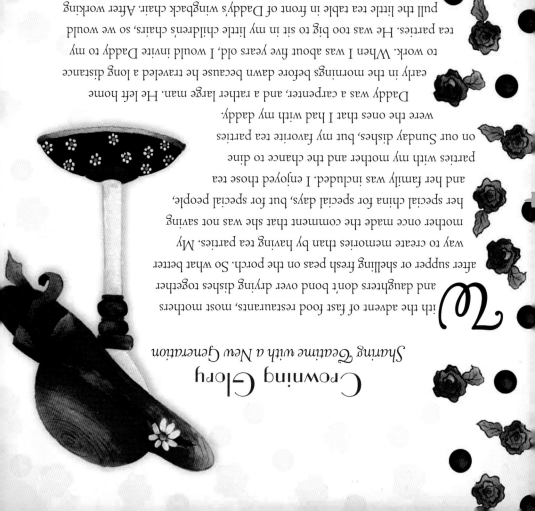

Crowning Glory
Sharing Teatime with a New Generation

ith the advent of fast food restaurants, most mothers and daughters don't bond over drying dishes together after supper or shelling fresh peas on the porch. So what better way to create memories than by having tea parties. My mother once made the comment that she was not saving her special china for special days, but for special people. And her family was included. I enjoyed those tea parties with my mother and the chance to dine on our Sunday dishes, but my favorite tea parties were the ones that I had with my daddy.

Daddy was a carpenter, and a rather large man. He left home early in the mornings before dawn because he traveled a long distance to work. When I was about five years old, I would invite Daddy to my tea parties. He was too big to sit in my little children's chairs, so we would pull the little tea table in front of Daddy's wingback chair. After working so hard all day long, I am sure he would have much rather settled in to read the evening newspaper, but I used my childhood tea set and served him bananas, raisins, and marshmallows. (I am sure none of his fellow workers were ever told of this.) He would ask me about my day, and I am sure I told him all about it. Out of the tiny Blue Willow teacups we drank our "tea" that was really ginger ale, and for a few moments I took notice that I had the treasure of his undivided attention. That was so many years ago. Today I visited my 92-year-old father in the hospital.

Health in Every Cup

Teas have all sorts of wonderful health benefits. Studies continue to show that something we like so well is actually good for us. Teas that are made from rose hips, the cranberry-sized red fruits that form on the rose bush after the flowers fade, are rich in Vitamin C.

Now I am the one who works all day and would enjoy a leisurely evening of reading. Upon entering his room he smiled. So feeble and frail, he couldn't sit in a chair, so I pulled mine next to him. The attendant had brought his supper and we both urged him to eat. He insisted sharing his tea with me, so I poured some into a cup. He asked me about my day, and I shared with him the day's work of running a business and running a family. Our roles were reversed. . . he looked at me, and in sharing our tea he took notice that he had a treasured moment of my undivided attention.

Life isn't a matter of milestones, but of moments.
Rose Kennedy

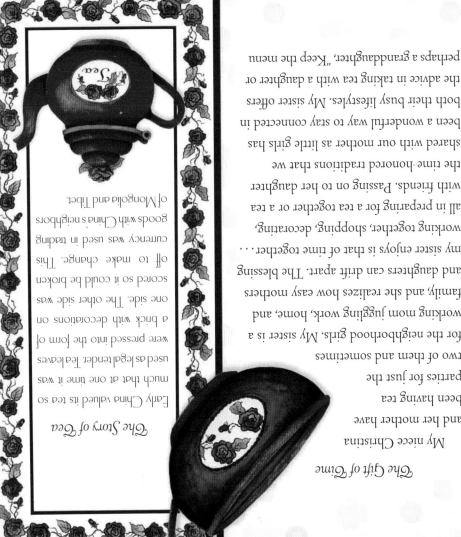

The Gift of Time

My niece Christina and her mother have been having tea parties for just the two of them and sometimes for the neighborhood girls. My sister is a working mom juggling work, home, and family, and she realizes how easy mothers and daughters can drift apart. The blessing my sister enjoys is that of time together... working together, shopping, decorating, all in preparing for a tea together or a tea with friends. Passing on to her daughter the time-honored traditions that we shared with our mother as little girls has been a wonderful way to stay connected in both their busy lifestyles. My sister offers the advice in taking tea with a daughter or perhaps a granddaughter, "Keep the menu

The Story of Tea

Early China valued its tea so much that at one time it was used as legal tender. Tea leaves were pressed into the form of a brick with decorations on one side. The other side was scored so it could be broken off to make change. This currency was used in trading goods with China's neighbors of Mongolia and Tibet.

Dressing Up for the Occasion

A chest or basket full of vintage "dress up" clothing provides a fun activity for a legacy tea. Hats are a very important part of tea party attire. You might even start the party by making hats to wear. Lots of costume jewelry (the more rhinestones the better), boas, and gloves make a tea party much more fun. Be sure and take lots of pictures using an instant camera or a digital camera (if you can make prints at home). Place the photos into inexpensive picture frames and you have sweet parting gifts that make a most memorable take-home favor.

simple. When leafing through the recipe books, remember that the most important thing you can make together is a memory."

I saw firsthand how important this was to hand down the tradition of taking tea together after visiting a friend in South Dakota. Gloria was a shop owner who shared my love for tea. She grew up having teas with her mother, grandmother, and her adored Great Aunt Mabel. The pretty dishes, the linens, the decorative plates and dainty teacups created a world she loved. At an early age she realized that the intricate little details make someone feel special. Tea parties became a treasured time simply because someone "took the

time." Gloria learned that the gift of hospitality was simply a gift of time.

Great Aunt Mabel never had any children, so she passed down her collection of dishes and tea party fare to Gloria. But, of course, she passed down more than that. Gloria inherited her aunts love of sharing, treasuring friendships, and giving graciously to those you love. Gloria learned well from her Aunt Mabel. . . . I was a guest at one of the annual High Teas that Gloria hosts for over 300 women.

Remember that the most important thing you can make together is a memory.

CHERYL JOHNSON

Children's Legacy Tea

Tea Cakes

Bread and Strawberry Butter Sandwiches

Chocolate Dipped Strawberries

Cambric Tea

Tea Cakes

Make miniature cupcakes as a perfect-for-small-hands "tea cake." Offer bread and butter sandwiches cut in cookie cutter shapes of hearts and flowers. To make a wonderful strawberry butter, soften a carton of whipped, unsalted butter. Mix with a jar of strawberry preserves. Spread on sandwiches. Garnish with a fresh picked, washed violet or pansy...they are edible too!

WELCOME LADIES

Chocolate Dipped Strawberries

one pint of fresh strawberries with caps and stems remaining

12 ounces semi-sweet chocolate

Rinse one pint of fresh strawberries and pat dry with paper towels. Leave the green caps and stems on. Line a cookie sheet with waxed paper. Melt 12 ounces of semi-sweet chocolate in double boiler over simmering water. Stir until melted. Hold the strawberry by the stem or leaf and dip only half of it into the chocolate. Let the excess drip off the berry, back into the chocolate, and lay it on the wax paper. Repeat until all the strawberries are dipped and store the cookie sheet in the refrigerator until ready to serve.

Cambric tea was hot water and milk,
with only a taste of tea in it,
but little girls felt grown-up
when their mothers
let them drink cambric tea.

LAURA INGALLS WILDER
The Long Winter

Cambric Tea

A child-size tea set is a must, for little hands need little cups and a teapot that is not too heavy when pouring. (What a wonderful gift to give a young hostess.) The tea itself could be an endless number of possibilities. Cambric tea was the traditional tea served in children's nurseries just before bedtime. It is simply milk with a spot of tea for color and you can add sugar to taste.

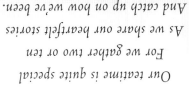

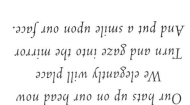

A Little Cup of Friendship Tea

Let us gather for a greeting
With our teacups filled with tea
And I'll tell you how important
Your friendship is to me.

Our hats up on our head now
We elegantly will place
Turn and gaze into the mirror
And put a smile upon our face.

Our teatime is quite special
For we gather two or ten
As we share our heartfelt stories
And catch up on how we've been.

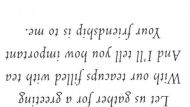

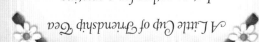

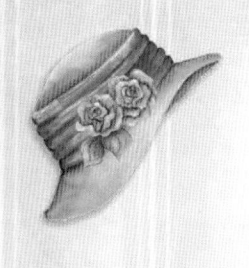

We share of all the happenings
Of each our busy lives
The daily goings on and on
All our blessings and our strife.

It may have been a week or two
Or just maybe yesterday
We give each other insights
Into our busy ways.

For time moves much too quickly
As we sit and drink our tea
May we pause for just a moment
And make a memory.

ALDA

Bibliography

Johnson, Dorthea, *The Little Book of Etiquette from the Protocol School of Washington* (Philadelphia: Running Press, 1997).

Pettigrew, Jane, *Design for Tea* (Gloucestershire: Sutton Publishing Limited, 2003).

Richardson, Bruce, *The Great Tea Rooms of America* (Perryville, KY: Benjamin Press, 2003).

Traditional Home Magazine (May 2001).

Thank you and appreciation to the following sources for the information they provided:

Tea Association of the U.S.A.
230 Park Avenue
New York, New York 10169

Tea Council of the U.S.A.
230 Park Avenue
New York, New York 10169